Caroline Walker Shelton, the only Walker sister to marry, poses with her children in front of a tulip pattern quilt.

© 2011 Great Smoky Mountains Association. All rights reserved.

Edited by Steve Kemp and Kent Cave
Cover and book design by Lisa Horstman

Cover image from GSMNP archives
Editorial assistance by Julie Brown and Valerie Polk

1 2 3 4 5 6 7 8 9 10

♲ Printed on recycled paper approved by the Forest Stewardship Council using vegetable-based inks.

ISBN 978-0-937207-68-0

Great Smoky Mountains Association is a private, nonprofit organization which supports the educational, scientific, and historical programs of Great Smoky Mountains National Park. To learn more about our publications, memberships, guided hikes, and other activities, please contact GSMA, 115 Park Headquarters Road, Gatlinburg, TN 37738. (865) 436-7318.
www.SmokiesInformation.org

All purchases benefit Great Smoky Mountains National Park.

Printed in the United States of America.

FSC
www.fsc.org

MIX
Paper from
responsible sources
FSC® C020656

Storied Stitches:
QUILTS AND COVERLETS
of the Smokies

by Rose Houk

People in the Great Smoky Mountains certainly knew thin times. But no matter how threadbare things might have gotten, they always had thick bedcovers to keep them warm at night. Quilts and coverlets made by hand were part of almost every mountain home.

Stitching quilts and weaving coverlets was a long-held tradition in the southern Appalachians. In the early 1800s, Cherokee women were spinning cotton and weaving cloth—some 584,000 yards of it a year by one estimation—while girls in mission schools sold their quilts for six or seven dollars. By the early 1900s, the director of a Gatlinburg school observed that "Many of the women make exquisite patchwork quilts, and some will make the hand woven coverlids and blankets."

While born of necessity, these handmade covers were things of beauty, created with care and love, and each and every one telling stories of people's lives.

Sarah Connelly, a spinner and weaver from North Carolina, seated in front of a quilt with a woven coverlet on her lap.

QUILTS

Detail from a Double Irish Chain pattern quilt in the Walker Sisters Collection, GSMNP.

IN ITS MOST FUNDAMENTAL FORM, a quilt is any three-layered sandwich of fabric–a top, an inner insulative stuffing, and a backing. The top may be made of a whole piece of cloth, but more often is of separate pieced or appliquéd blocks sewn together. Once it's finished, the three layers are assembled, stretched out on a frame, and stitched through all the layers to keep the filling from shifting. Thus, "quilt" is both a noun and a verb. It is a thing, and it is a process.

Quilts and quilting have deep roots in history. The word comes from the Latin, *culcita*, for stuffed sock or mattress, and its earliest forms were seen several thousand years before Christ. Warriors in the Crusades wore quilted armor, and by the fourteenth century people in Europe were using quilts of silk, wool, linen, and imported chintzes as bedcovers. Quilts were stashed in the holds of ships that came to the American colonies, and by Revolutionary War times the new country already had its own quilt industry.

Quilts, and the know-how to make them, came with the earliest pioneers who swept through the gaps to settle the Great Smoky Mountains in the 1700s. With the old patterns and aged, soft colors, these handcrafted covers nearly symbolize early frontier life. Quilts were among the few belongings the Cherokee took with them on the Trail of Tears in 1838-1839, when thousands of native people were evicted from the mountains. During the Civil War, slaves and free blacks made quilts, and ladies aid societies stitched them for soldiers and the war effort. Fancy "crazy quilts" caught on during Victorian times. And during the 1920s and 1930s, a quilt revival gripped the entire nation. To one degree or another, quilters in the Smoky Mountains took part in all these trends. But more than their counterparts elsewhere in the nation, they never really stopped quilting.

As John Rice Irwin, founder of the Museum of Appalachia in Norris, Tennessee, has observed, even after inexpensive, readymade blankets could be purchased, quilts remained popular in the southern Appalachians. In fact, "old time quilting never altogether ceased" here, he said. During his years spent traveling deep into the hills and hollows, Irwin talked with many quilters and amassed an impressive quilt collection. It was the grandmothers who were quilting, he said. One lady he met had made 100 quilts, and she was 100 years old. The finest quilts would be packed away and brought out only

Left: A cushion created in the Crazy Quilt pattern from the Walker Sisters Collection, GSMNP.

Right: A small scale Log Cabin and String pattern doll quilt. The quilt's three layers are tied, not quilted.

on special occasions, but basically "everybody had quilts." Irwin's mother and grandmother quilted too, and theirs were put to good use in the house he grew up in. Without heat in the bedrooms, even when temperatures dipped toward zero, he recalled being "perfectly comfortable" snuggled beneath "four or five of those old handmade quilts."

Besides their use as warm bedcovers, quilts were put to other purposes too. Pallets of them were stacked up and slept on. Quilts were used as curtains to keep out dust. They covered canned goods and barrels of pickled beans to keep them from freezing. They were laid on the ground for the children to play on while a mother worked in the garden. Quilts were often used as the backdrop for family portraits. Sometimes they were items of barter, used to settle debts. And in a few cases, quilts were even used to wrap the dead.

Today, quilts remain as tangible records of the most important family and personal events. They were made for newborns and newlyweds, sons, daughters, and grandchildren; as gifts for a church minister; or donations to charitable and political causes. Eliot Wigginton, editor of the popular *Foxfire* books, said it so well: "A quilt is something human. Quilts were handmade by people for people. Every phase of their production was permeated by giving and sharing."

WHEN A WOMAN'S WORK FOR THE DAY was done—cooking, canning, hoeing the garden, tending to the children—she could finally sit a spell, bring out her sewing basket, and enjoy the peace and quiet of evening, as the mountainsides turned to gold, the clouds shaded into peach, and fireflies blinked on like tiny stars. Or in winter, she could let the quilt frame down from the ceiling, while the wind howled outside in the early darkness, satisfied that she was making something her family truly needed.

Necessity was always the basic motivation for quilting, and the great majority of quilts made in the Smokies were utilitarian—not always beautiful or painstakingly constructed, but eminently practical and useful. "All they thought about was keeping warm," said one woman. Yet some took quilting to another level, applying creativity and talent to make an heirloom of lasting beauty.

Beyond that, quilting provided an opportunity for socializing. Unlike most other chores that were done alone, quilting offered a respectable excuse to get together and accomplish a useful task. Family, friends, and neighbors were

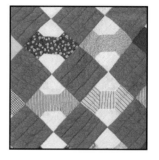

Detail from a Bow Tie pattern quilt from the Walker Sisters Collection.

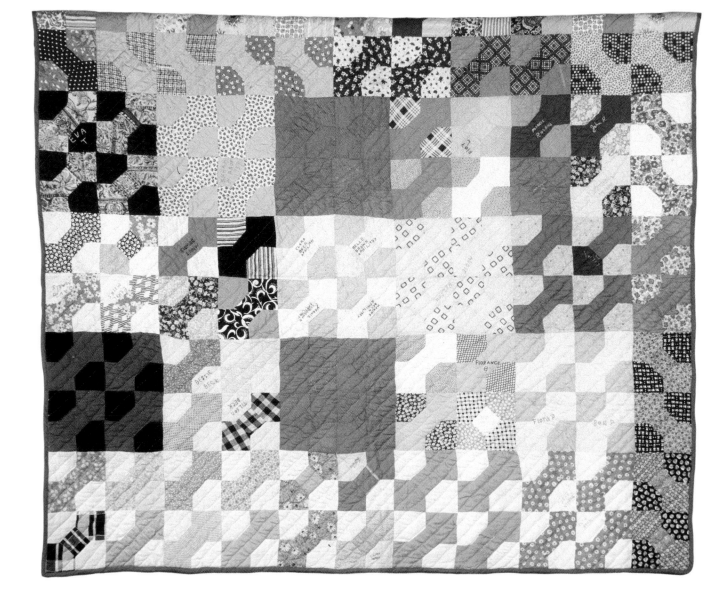

Tow String Church Quilt

Stored in the Mountain Heritage Center at Western Carolina University in Cullowhee is the "Tow String Church quilt." It's a special quilt that carries a meaningful story of persistence among a group of people of the Great Smoky Mountains.

The quilt is pieced in a bowtie pattern in prints and solids of blue, orange, apricot, green, purple, and gold, with a floral backing fabric and blue binding. It is hand quilted. Embroidered on the patches are the names of church members and the quiltmakers—Bessie Beck, Maggie Rowland, Maudie Dowdle, and others. Fortunately, they not only signed their names but some included the month and year, April 1937. So for this quilt, we have rare information of exactly when it was made.

This friendship quilt was a going away gift for the minister of the Tow String Missionary Baptist Church, located near Smokemont on the North Carolina side of the Smokies. As Great Smoky Mountains National Park was being carved out of private lands, the people had to move away. But they weren't going without their church. They physically moved the building, board by board, to a new location and rebuilt it just outside the park's southern boundary.

After more than seventy years, the old box-style church was rotting on its foundation. So members of the congregation decided to build a brand new church, with their own hands and in the same spot. The neat-trimmed, spanking white house of worship is in regular use today.

The quilt, meanwhile, had gone to the pastor's widow, who then passed it on to the Beck family, believing it would have more meaning to them. A descendant donated it to the heritage center. Now it's in safe keeping, and the Tow String community still has its church.

The Bowtie pattern quilt made by church members of the Tow String Missionary Baptist Church.

Above: A commemorative 1904 Thanksgiving quilt from the Walker Sisters Collection.

Right: a detail from a Friendship Ring quilt made by Sarah Jane Stooksbury Irwin.

invited to a quilting bee or party—in fact, it was a social slight not to receive an invitation. They gathered in church basements or in someone's home, pulled chairs around the quilt frame, took up needle and thread, and did the handstitching. While the work was being done, of course there was plenty of time for the women to catch up on the latest news and gossip. These community efforts were often undertaken to finish a quilt for a gift—for the church preacher, for a family setting up a new home, or for an eligible young man. Still quilting bees were enough like parties that one young Tennessee woman wondered in her diary whether it would be appropriate to join a quilting on Christmas Day, because it seemed "a little like profanation." In any event, quilting bees allowed completion of a big project that would have taken many more hours for an individual working alone.

Quilts are cloaked in superstition too, like "shake the cat" for example. When a quilt came off the frame, the unmarried women went outdoors, put a wary feline in the center of the quilt, held onto the corners and bounced the nervous animal into the air. Whoever the cat landed closest to would be the next to wed. Other superstitions were based more on religion. Never quilt on Sunday. Or, be sure to include a purposeful imperfection in the quilt so as not to tempt God.

Many common threads run through stories about how a person learned to quilt. Eva Myers was born in 1930 in the Jakes Creek area of the Great Smokies, one of the last children born in what would become the national park. "My first memory is sitting under a quilt, I would have been eight or ten," Eva recalled. She sat on the floor beneath a quilt stretched on a frame, as her mother, grandmother, and aunt did the handquilting. Now in her eighties, Eva keeps her hands busy all the time, finishing quilts on her own or with a group at the Sevierville Senior Center.

Right: Ellen Ogle with a few of her quilts.

Top: A quilt made from an old pair of Ellen's husband's denim overalls.

Bottom: A Spider Web quilt.

Ellen Ogle of Gatlinburg, Tennessee, knew exactly when she made her first quilt. She was eleven years old, she said, when she cut out 10-by-12-inch squares of cloth and sewed them together by the light of a kerosene lamp. Now a retired ranger for the national park, Ellen gets her ailing husband settled for the night, then quilts into the wee hours of the morning. "The Lord gives us the strength to do what we have to do," she said simply. When asked how many quilts she's made in her life, Ellen responded: "I would say a good 500."

Iva McKee, who "grew up way back in the mountains," started quilting when she was a little girl too, learning from her mother, grandmother, and aunts. She still has her first quilt top, of colorful two-inch cotton squares, "just scraps from mama's quilts." Though Iva stopped quilting for a while as an adult, she took it up again and owns a busy quilt shop in Sevierville, Tennessee.

Esta Laney of Bryson City, North Carolina, echoed these early lessons. A child when she started quilting, Esta also learned from her mother. When "life was good," she said, they purchased fabric, but mostly "we just used what we had." She remembered that her mother's quilt frame hung from hooks on the ceiling, but it was put up "when the menfolk came in." Today, Esta's frame is set up in her small living room, her tools as simple as masking tape and ruler to mark her quilting lines. She's passed on her talents to her daughter, Linda Stephenson, who said she only quilts by the book. But the results of Linda's handwork are equally striking.

By and large, women were the ones who quilted. A few men did engage in the craft, even though not a lot would admit it. An exception was Alex Stewart, an acquaintance of John Rice Irwin's. A true mountain man, Alex was a master of many useful skills—cooper, carpenter, well-digger, stone mason,

Album Block quilt detail from the Walker Sisters Collection.

blacksmith, and beekeeper. But at his 92nd birthday party, he surprised Irwin when he mentioned he also knew how to quilt. "You get me a needle and thread and I'll show you whether I can quilt or not," Alex declared. Then he commenced to show everyone how it was done.

The Walker sisters of Little Greenbrier, who gained a lifelong lease to remain on their family land long after creation of Great Smoky Mountains National Park, were well-known quilters. In fact, one of the oldest quilts in the park collection is one of theirs. It was made of striped cotton and wool cloth, possibly from an apron or skirt. Those strips were alternated with crazy-style pieced strips. Quilt historian Merikay Waldvogel said this technically would be called a "strip quilt," though the Walkers might have called it a "linsey" quilt for the thick, handwoven cotton and wool material they cut up and reused in it. Waldvogel dated the quilt to around 1890.

Strip, or string, quilting was popular among early-day Smokies quilters. Scrap cloth was cut into narrow rectangles and stitched onto a foundation of paper, often old newspaper. The strips were then sewn together by hand into blocks, the paper trimmed away, and the full quilt assembled. Sometimes the maker left the paper in place, little knowing that if it carried a date it would let future quilt historians discover the textile's age.

Appliqué was another technique. It involved cutting cloth into pictorial shapes, turning under a narrow hem around each piece, then embroidering the cutouts onto a square of fabric. Many a little girl received a Dutch Doll appliqué quilt, and Eva Myers proudly did one in pink for her great granddaughter. The richness of wildflowers in the mountains also inspired patterns for appliqué.

By far, the preferred method among Smokies quilters was piecing, or patchwork. This is probably what most people think of when they envision

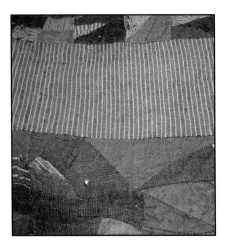

Detail of the Walker sisters' linsey quilt, one of the oldest quilts in the Great Smoky Mountains National Park collection.

Linda Stephenson and her mother, Esta
Laney, with their extensive family
heirloom quilt collection.

Above: Esta stitches her current quilt, an
appliqué Butterfly Quilt pattern.

String quilt detail, by Martha King, ca. 1880, TN.

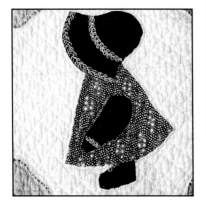

Dutch Girl appliqué quilt detail, by Sarah Jane Stooksbury Irwin, ca. 1890, TN.

Bear Paw or Wandering Foot patchwork detail, by Winifred Mewborn, ca. 1918-20, NC.

an old-fashioned quilt. Basically, a pattern was selected or invented; templates of paper or cardboard made; the templates laid on fabric and traced around; then the squares, triangles, or curved pieces were cut out with scissors. The pieces were then seamed together to make a square block. A number of blocks were put together to make a quilt top, and perfectly matched "points" and corners were tribute to a quilter's skill. If she was precise from the beginning in cutting and piecing, everything came together well. If not, as with carpentry, the errors only compounded as the assembly continued.

More than one person might wonder why anyone would go to all the trouble. As one quilter from Pigeon Forge shared, "Papa would say… 'You go buy all this fabric, cut it and just sew it back together.'" But anyone making that statement obviously had never been infected with quilting fever!

The number of patchwork patterns is nearly endless—favorite and common among mountain quilters were Nine Patch, Irish Chain, Flying Geese, Bear Paw, Maple Leaf, Grandmother's Flower Garden, Double Wedding Ring, and Carolina Lily, emblematic of its namesake state. The Log Cabin pattern might be considered an icon of the Smokies. But, it originated in the 1840s in another part of the country and was widespread for 150 years, and remains one of the most beloved patterns in quiltdom. It consists of a center square, usually red to symbolize a hearth, surrounded by narrow strips of lights and darks; arrangements of the log cabin blocks result in almost infinite variations on the theme. Even the simplest natural feature could inspire a quilter. For Esta Laney, the backlit spider webs that tufted the grass on the hillside above her house might have led to a quilt that she proudly held up, made in what she called the Spider Web pattern.

Before printed patterns were available, quiltmakers would make a sketch or a cloth sample to go by. Esta Laney said sometimes they just saw a picture and went home and figured out how to make it. Quilters frequently copied and traded patterns, and rarely discarded them. Ellen Ogle pulled out a box with hundreds of patterns in it, all neatly organized and labeled. Some were her mother's, cut out of the church bulletin. Soon, though, quilt patterns could be purchased from magazines and newspapers. *Godey's Lady's Book* was one of the first to offer patchwork patterns, from the 1830s to 1890s. *Ladies' Home Journal, Southern Woman's Magazine, Good Housekeeping,* and several others also included them.

But choosing a pattern was only the beginning. Next came the choice and combinations of fabrics and colors—of solids, prints, light and darks, homespun, calico, wool, or velvet—for the blocks, border, background, and binding. For many, this presented the real delight of the craft. For others it was seeing the patterns come together, or doing the hand quilting. Through its several layers, quilting afforded mountain women a true creative outlet. Otherwise restrained by gender, education, and workload, in quilting they could break free and explore colors and shapes in an unfettered way. Some said they saw a quilt in their dreams, then undertook to translate it into reality. They introduced symbolism, focused more on beauty than utility, and let their voices be heard through pattern and color. Though few quilters had any kind of formal art training, some undeniably succeeded in raising quilting to an artform.

Patchwork certainly held practical advantages, mainly that the blocks could be pieced separately, picked up and worked on as time allowed, and took up little space. For mountain women, patchwork quilts presented the ideal opportunity to make do with what was on hand, using and reusing every single available scrap of cloth. Store-bought fabric was expensive and not always available to Smokies residents. So once a shirt, a pair of pants, or other clothing

Spider Web quilt detail, by Esta Laney, ca. 1950, TN.

Carolina Lily detail, by Mrs. Murphy Allred, ca. 1870, NC.

Log Cabin in squares and diamonds quilt, ca. 1870.

A small sampling of quilter Ellen Ogle's quilt patterns. Hundreds of them are organized and labeled inside a large box.

became threadbare, they were cut into shapes for a quilt block. Many people smile when they see in a quilt a recognizable piece of fabric from what was once mama's dress or apron.

For a great portion of quilting's history, all this meticulous work was done entirely by hand. But by 1846, a revolutionary device was introduced in the United States. The sewing machine promised huge time-savings for seamstresses and quilters. Though quilt pieces were still cut by hand, the "iron seamstress" offered much greater speed in piecing. The new machines were considered "valuable aids to female industry," and by 1860 *Godey's* magazine declared that "In quilting, and all kinds of stitching, they seem indispensable." The Walker sisters had a Seamstress brand treadle machine, reportedly the second one ever purchased in Sevier County. (In 1898, that machine sold for seven to fourteen dollars.) A foot-operated treadle machine didn't require electricity–a boon to people in the far reaches of the Smoky Mountains in the early days–and some quilters still prefer a treadle because they feel it gives them more control. Yet purists remain, Esta Laney among them, who think sewing machines are more trouble than they're worth. Esta still prefers to complete every part of her quilts by hand, and would like to see that method come back. "It's just a good thing to do," she concluded.

By the mid-nineteenth century, other big changes strongly influenced quilting. Manufactured cloth, along with machine prints and chemical dyes, were more readily available, brought into the mountains by railroads and traveling peddlers with their "rolling stores." North Carolina, especially, had a thriving domestic textile industry that could meet the demand for cloth. By the last quarter of the nineteenth century, machine-made bed coverings were used in many American households with the advent of power machines and the industrialized needle trade. But, home quilting was still the common practice in the southern mountains. Nearly every farm family made quilts of everyday materials for everyday use.

The inner stuffing held between the quilt top and the backing was the batting, or "batten" as it's sometimes called. In ancient times the filler consisted of leaves, grass, or feathers. As quilts took their modern form, it was wool or cotton. For warmth on cold winter nights in the mountains, a quilt could contain six pounds of cotton batting. Even in the cooler climate of the Smoky Mountains, a few people did raise cotton, among them the Walker sisters who also owned a small, ingenious, hand-operated cotton gin. And no doubt they did as Eva Myers when she was a young girl, sitting by the fireplace removing the seeds and bolls before using the raw cotton for quilt batting. If homegrown cotton batts were used, the cotton clumped up and residual plant parts remained that can still be seen when a quilt is held up to the light. Occasionally, an old blanket or even a quilt that had grown a little "raggedy" would become batting for a new quilt.

A huge advance in batting came from two enterprising men. In 1846 George Stearns and Seth Foster, husbands of quilters, experimented with glazed sheets of cotton and eventually produced "cotton wadding." Stearns & Foster Company's Mountain Mist batting has been a staple of quilters

The large collection of family quilts owned by Linda Stephenson and Esta Laney. Many are made from feed sacks.

Our Father which art in heaven, Hallowed be thy name, thy Kingdom come, Thy will be done in earth, as it is in heaven, Give us this day our daily bread, And Forgive us our debts, as we forgive Our debtors, and lead us not into Temptation, but deliver us from Evil. For thine is the kingdom, And the power, and the glory, For ever. Amen.

God B O Fami

Glory to God

Mother Home in Heaven

Remember Me

During the last two decades of the nineteenth century, crazy quilts represented a short-lived but important "craze." They diverged from more traditional patchwork, with no real pattern to the piecing, just irregular shapes and sizes of fabric—often silks and velvets—randomly arranged, with the edges overlaid with elaborate embroidery. Many were gorgeous works of art. But in the Smoky Mountains only a few people made them, most likely because they neither had money to buy such luxurious fabrics nor parlors in which to display them.

Among those who did try their hand at a crazy quilt was John Rice Irwin's grandmother, Sarah Jane Stooksbury Irwin. "Granny" Irwin's crazy quilt, made in the 1890s, was brought out only around Christmas, used as a bedcover through the holidays, then put away for another year. It was made of more common fabrics but was lavishly embroidered. The

Lord's Prayer was stitched in the center patch, while roosters, cows, a horse, and a fiddle were added. A few friends included their initials or names, making this an example of what was known as a "friendship" quilt.

Like most quilters, Sarah Jane didn't sign her name on this quilt. But one rectangle on the far edge carried the words "Remember Me." This poignant phrase may have been the quilter's expression of desire for lasting recognition of her labor of love.

Left: Sarah Jane Stooksbury Irwin's lavishly embroidered Christmas quilt.

Above: John Rice Irwin at the Museum of Appalachia with more of his family's heirloom quilts.

ever since (and conveniently, their packaging also carried quilt patterns).

Once the three layers of a quilt were basted together and stretched on a frame, it was time to apply the hand stitching—when "quilt" becomes a verb, and when a quilt takes on texture and dimension. As one writer put it, a quilt became a "canvas" to show off a person's finest sewing skills. The hand quilting pattern was drawn on the top with chalk or other removable marker. On many mountain quilts, it was a simple fan design or diagonal lines; or the handwork would be done "in the ditch" along the seams of a patchwork block. In some very fine pieces, the motifs grew stunningly elaborate. The tiny running stitch was done with special needles called "sharps." Many people judged a quilter's skill by the number of stitches per inch, 10 to 12 being one standard; others noted that uniformity of the stitches was more important than fineness. Sometimes a quicker method, called tufting, or tying, was used to secure the three layers. This was common among Smokies quilters, especially on everyday quilts, but sometimes even tufting took on elaborate form.

By the early twentieth century, growing prosperity allowed more and more people to engage in quilting. For women in the coves and valleys of the Smoky Mountains, as well as those living in big cities, quilts were elevated from functional bed coverings to items of home décor. Even as the Great Depression gripped the country, there was a quilt revival. People had gone from the darker browns and blues of older days to soft pastels. And into the Depression, they continued to select the pastels, seemingly in denial, or defiance, of the harsh economic conditions. In her fascinating book, *Soft Covers for Hard Times*, Merikay Waldvogel wrote that during these years quilting was rediscovered by people beyond the circle of regional, traditional quilters. Even after the stock market crash in 1929, "The quiltmaking frenzy continued unabated," she stated.

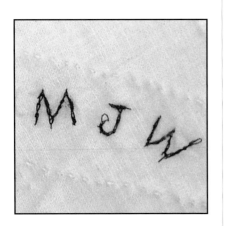

Initials MJW (Margaret Jane Walker) stitched on the back of a quilt.

*The Seamstress brand
treadle machine owned by
the Walker sisters.*

But, and this is the key, magazines and newspapers gained unprecedented influence, resulting in a "homogenization" of patterns that quilters everywhere could order. They could also get kits complete with pre-cut fabric and patterns. The *Knoxville News-Sentinel* offered "The Wonder Package," a cold transfer process for appliqué and patchwork squares that could be used repeatedly. A person could get it by mail for a dollar, or stop by in person and get the package for only 88 cents. And in 1933 Sears, Roebuck held a nationwide quilt contest at the Chicago World's Fair that raised the ante for quilters, offering significant cash prizes. Quilters in the Smoky Mountains had access to, and

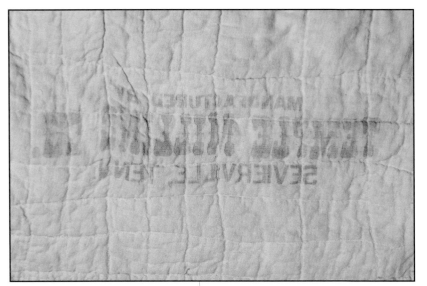

This detail from one of Ellen Ogle's feed sack quilts bears the Temple Milling Co. stamp.

participated in, all the same materials, media, and contests.

The Depression years were also the time when people were moving out of the Great Smoky Mountains as their properties were purchased to form the new national park. But they didn't go far away, and in the communities hard against the park they resettled and continued to live much as they always had—raising and preserving their own food and making quilts of whatever they had at hand. Readily available were the plain cotton sacks in which they got their flour and cornmeal, chicken and calf feed, sugar and tobacco. Such sacks had been around for quite a while from places like Temple Milling in Sevierville and White Lily in Knoxville, and frugal women had already been using them in quilts. Ellen Ogle held up several of those quilts stacked in her bedroom closet. "Mama always made our clothes out of feed sacks and what was left over she made into quilts," she added. Women worked furiously to remove the company trademark from the cloth bag with lye soap and bleach, but no matter how much they scrubbed, the ink often would not come out completely. So they'd turn the sack over and use it on a quilt back. Eva Myers showed a quilt with a sack whose priceless logo fortunately had not been removed—it was "Roy Acuff's Own Flour, Specially Blended for Roy Acuff By Cherokee Mills, Nashville, Tenn."—with Roy's likeness alongside a WSM radio microphone. Realizing the demand, milling companies began to produce cloth sacks in colorful prints—pretty enough to use in the patchwork on a quilt top—and with removable labels. Esta Laney said her mother went to the store and traded for sacks so she would have enough of the same print to use in a quilt. They would also use Rit or Diamond dyes to color plain sacks. And Esta and others mentioned pulling out the chainstitched string from the bags to use for the handquilting. Nothing went to waste for those frugal women during those frugal times.

By the 1960s and 1970s, cloth sacks had gone the way of draft horses and draw knives, replaced mostly with paper. In rural east Tennessee and western North Carolina, modern machine fabric remnants from textile mills were used in basic tied quilts. But in these decades another quilt revival was underway, with strikingly different motivations. Part of this resurgence was caught up in the back-to-the-land movement, an urge by a new generation to live the supposed simpler, self-sustaining lifestyle of the elders. But mostly it had to do with a new view of quilts as decorative home furnishings and as wall hangings. Quilts were more frequently being custom made of color-coordinated fabrics, and some were artistic expressions never intended for ordinary use. Older quilts became collector's items, and museums started to curate and show them. With the introduction of new tools and materials, such as rotary cutters, polyester batting, and computerized sewing machines, the art and craft of quilting has been embraced by millions of people who started learning to quilt, buying supplies, joining groups, and attending shows.

By the mid 1980s, quilt historians in several states, including Tennessee and North Carolina, undertook exhaustive quilt survey projects, with the hope of obtaining "images of everyday life in America of a time now past." Project organizers went into towns and cities in every county, inviting people to bring in their quilts for thorough documentation. More than 1,400 pre-1930s quilts were recorded in Tennessee, where Cocke and Sevier counties,

A baby quilt from the Walker Sisters Collection.

Top: A treasured Double Wedding Ring antique quilt from Maria Holloway's collection.

Bottom: The feed sack quilt found by Maria Holloway's husband, John, in a Cosby creek.

neighboring the Great Smokies, were the best represented. In North Carolina another 10,000 were recorded, which included quilts made through 1975. In both states, the lion's share was patchwork quilts, the style favored in the Great Smoky Mountains for a very long time. Now there are also events called "bed turnings," like the one at the Pigeon Forge Quilt Fest each year. People bring in their quilts, and fifty or more of the quilts are stacked on top of a bed, each one examined and documented for those believed to be at least fifty years old. These are the old quilts found in someone's attic or hope chest, now cherished heirlooms, in patterns and pieces that hold the threads of people's life stories.

For Maria Holloway, a very special quilt holds her favorite life story. Maria has seen many fine quilts in her day, and she knows the standards used to judge them. But the one she holds most dear is just a plain country quilt that appeared completely by accident. One morning her husband John was walking across the bridge over the creek that flows through their land in Cosby, Tennessee. He thought he saw a feed sack washing downstream, but when he pulled it out with a rake he found instead a full pieced quilt. He and Maria washed and dried it, and discovered it had been made with feed sacks, in pleasing light green squares and pastel butterflies. A simple, basic quilt made by someone to keep them warm, but that surely brought pride in the making. But Maria had to ask herself, was it really an accident that the quilt appeared when and how it did? She took it as a sign that she and John would stay and establish Holloway's Quilt Shop in Cosby, right on the edge of Great Smoky Mountains National Park.

Maria Holloway in her shop with two of many quilts of her own design.

Maria and her granddaughter work on a quilt in progress.

COVERLETS

A young Appalachian girl sitting at a loom with a shuttle in her hand, ca. 1930.

THERE IS A LOT OF MUSIC in the weaving of cloth. A weaver seated at the loom worked the foot pedals like a pipe organ, and pulled the beater bar with a soft, steady rhythm. So mesmerizing was the process, she'd start humming or singing an old ballad without even thinking about it. Weaving was hypnotic. Hours would fly by at the loom, as the interlocked threads magically emerged in an intricately patterned piece of cloth.

Weaving—the process by which threads of two elements are interlaced at right angles—extends back into the dimmest recesses of human endeavor. Ten thousand years, at least, probably longer. It was like the discovery of fire. By plaiting together strands of almost any material—bark, grass, stems—people could make mats, baskets, bags, rope, sandals, and all sorts of useful items.

Using fibers of dogbane, mulberry root bark, and even buffalo hair, the Cherokee in the southern mountains had practiced what is known as finger weaving long before European contact. Master weaver Karen George, who learned it in school when she was a teenager, works to keep the traditional craft alive and gives demonstrations at the Oconaluftee Indian Village in Cherokee, North Carolina. Finger weaving does not use a loom. Instead, strands of yarn are measured out and attached to a wooden stick. The strands hang down to make a warp, and using only hands, no shuttles or bobbins, a weaver pulls the individual strands under and over each other to form a tight braid. Striking diagonal, chevron, and arrowhead designs are held in the weaver's mind, and the combination of colors makes each piece unique. With the arrival of Euro-Americans, handspun wool yarn in brighter colors was adopted. Karen said she often uses red, dark blue, black, and white, and also incorporates

Velvet Rose   Dolly Pratt's Coverlet   Whig Rose

Lovers Knot   Double Chariot Wheels   Double Compass

PATTERNS OF WEAVING

Sample weaving patterns displayed on a card.

Master weaver Karen George shows the technique of finger weaving, which uses no loom.

beads into her work. A two- to three-inch wide belt will take about sixty strands of yarn and five days to finish. Beaded pieces require a couple of weeks. Her belts and sashes are used mostly by traditional Cherokee dancers.

Meanwhile, others started to spin yarn and found ways to keep vertical strands under tension while weaving horizontal threads through them. With that came the manufacture of cloth. The Scots-Irish were industrious, prosperous weavers who brought their skill across the ocean to their new home in the southern Appalachian Mountains. They grew the raw materials, spun the yarn, and wove on handlooms, thus nurturing the craft of weaving from the earliest days of Euro-American settlement in the Great Smoky Mountains. A big wooden loom out on the front porch of a cabin in the summer was as common a sight as a springhouse or a mule. What they wove on those looms—beautiful bed-sized coverlets—were the highest expression of their craft.

Weaving is an altogether different activity than quilting. Weaving is done alone, while quilting sometimes has a social side to it. It requires a loom, and is far more physical and far less mobile. Some people did engage in both quilting and weaving. One was Elizabeth Cogdill Reagan, known to everyone at the Arrowmont School in Gatlinburg as "Aunt Lizzie." In the 1930s, then in her seventies, Aunt Lizzie laid out scraps of blue and brown handwoven swatches and embroidered them into a crazy quilt. When she died in 1946, the quilt was found in a trunk she left to her granddaughter. But Aunt Lizzie may have been an exception, because more typically a person chose one or the other of these crafts. There was just something about weaving that appealed to some people.

Normally, though, a woven coverlet didn't in any way resemble a quilt. The creation of a coverlet, also known as a "kiver" or "coverlid," was a complex task. It demanded detailed planning and several preliminary steps before a person ever sat down at the loom and actually wove. First, yarn had to be made. In the early days in the Smokies, people raised their own flax, some grew cotton, and some had sheep for wool.

Flax was planted, harvested, bundled, and spread out to "ret" or rot. The

A woven coverlet pillowcase with burlap backing from the GSMNP collection.

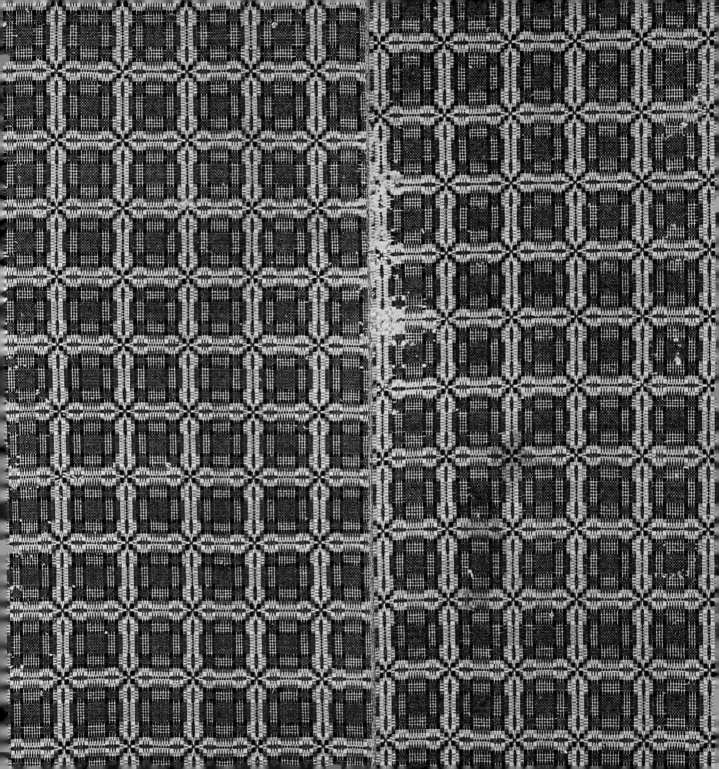

The Indigo Dye Pot

Many traditional woven coverlets contained blue as one of the two colors. And spinners and weavers went to great lengths to gain a rich blue from a natural source, the indigo plant. By all accounts, producing this dye was as much art as science, and involved the alchemy of the indigo dye pot. Frances Goodrich, in her book *Mountain Homespun*, goes into detail on how to go about it:

"A large iron pot...is the first requisite in the process. It is well if the pot has been used before for blue." The old recipe for the "blue pot" then called for warm water, two ounces of indigo "in a little sack," two ounces of madder, a teacup or two handfuls of wheat bran, and ½ pint of drip lye, enough to make the bran "feel slick or till water has a sweet taste." Soak indigo in the sack for about twelve hours, rub part of it into the water, add madder (fresh roots best), then the bran and lye. The pot was to be kept warm until the dye bath foams and turns green, and gives off an unforgettable fermented odor. Dip the yarn and hold up in the air until the desired degree of blueness is achieved.

A woman and two small boys work the dye pot in Madison County, NC in the 1920s.

This nineteenth century coverlet (front side at far left; back side at near left) made by an unidentified weaver is a variation of Catalpa Flower. It is in two colors: a blue indigo dyed wool thread and a brilliant red thread.

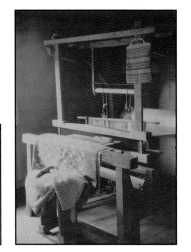

Clockwise from bottom left: A Lover's Knot coverlet; a flax hatchel; a weaving loom with an overhead beater; Elmeda Walker spinning on a big wheel ca. 1900; Elizabeth Cogdill Reagan, also known as "Aunt" Lizzie, holding two hand cards, ca. 1930.

coarse fibers were broken; "scotched" or bruised; "heckled" with a comb to separate the fibers; then spun on a low spinning wheel. The fine linen thread commonly was interwoven with wool to make the fabric called linsey-woolsey. Cotton involved a similar process of planting, harvesting, carding, and spinning. To obtain wool, sheep were sheared in the spring and sometimes again in early fall. The Walker sisters of Little Greenbrier were also accomplished weavers, who wove coverlets on a loom made by their father, John N. Walker. The women raised their own sheep, and as one person remarked, "any one of them can catch a buck or ewe, hogtie it and hoist it, bleating and kicking, to the rack where they do the shearing." A single sheep might yield about a pound of wool. After shearing, the raw wool or fleece was washed in warm water with lye soap, dried, hand carded, and formed into loose rolls called rolag ready for spinning. Cotton and wool, as opposed to flax, were spun on a "high" or "walking" wheel. It could take the output of six spinners to supply enough yarn for one weaver. Later, many mountain weavers bought machine-spun yarn made at Eureka Cotton Mills in Englewood, Tennessee.

A walking wheel from the GSMNP collection.

Before the days of commercial products, natural or vegetable dyes had to be prepared if colored yarn was desired. Bark, berries, roots, flowers, and mosses were gathered, soaked, and simmered in a dye bath. Walnut hulls gave a rich brown, pokeberries a red or pink, touch-me-not for orange, and yellow overcolored with hickory or black oak bark yielded green. A mordant such as alum or copper would be added to set the colors.

When enough yarn was wound onto bobbins, the warp, or vertical, threads were wound onto pegs in even lengths. Then it was time to "dress the loom," a laborious but critical step. Each warp thread was passed through the reed and then following the particular pattern, through the

Above: Riley and Eliza Fox.
Right: From the March 2,
1930 edition of the Knoxville
Sunday Journal.

Mountain Women Advertise Park In Big Cities Of America With Their Looms And Spinning Wheels

Mrs. Riley Fox, Mrs. Finley Mast do the Weaving; Mrs. Owenby Does the Talking.

By CARRIE C. CALLAWAY.

Since the Great Smoky Mountain National park has actually been created, and the nucleus of this playground for Eastern America was deeded to the United States government, much has been said about advertising the region to the country at large. A telling piece of advertising for this section, which, although it is in the nature of a by-product is none the less effective, is being undertaken, at this time, by three native mountain women.

These women are: Mrs. Allie Owenby, of Gatlinburg, to whom is due the credit of reviving the homespun period of pioneer days in her own neighborhood; Mrs. Riley Fox, of Walden's Creek, near the foot of Mt. LeConte, the king of the Smokies, who is the mother of eleven daughters, all of whom she has supported by her weaving, and Mrs. Finley Mast, of Valley Crucis, N. C., a master weaver, famous throughout the entire Appalachian region for her coverlets, having made both coverlets and rugs for the White House in the days of Mrs. Woodrow Wilson's regime.

Giving Demonstrations.

These women left Knoxville last Friday for a tour of six large cities, where, in a leading department store, in each city, they will stage a demonstration of weaving and other handcrafts, as these arts were carried on in the days of Bettie Ross. Their itinerary was arranged and their engagements, for putting on the demonstrations, were made by Frank E. Rudd, of Louisville, Ky., manufacturer of coverlets, in cotton and rayon. Mr. Rudd's coverlets are exact reproductions of the patterns woven on hand-looms in Revolutionary times.

Take Loom With Them.

The party will be gone some six weeks, stopping for one week in each city. The cities to be visited on the trip are Indianapolis, Pittsburgh, St. Louis, Minneapolis, Cincinnati, and Chicago. In each of these cities they have an engagement with a large department store, to show the public how weaving was done generations ago, on old-fashioned, hand-made looms. The women are taking with them a loom that is, nobody knows how old, and that was owned by Mrs. Fox's great-grandmother. They are also taking a spinning wheel, flax wheel, several pieces of old-fashioned, hand-made furniture, including a spool bed, and numerous coverlets, illustrating popular patterns.

Realistic Atmosphere.

In the stores, where the demonstrations are put on, a scene representing a typical mountain cabin interior is set up. This is done un-

Promoters of Mountain Industry

In the Boston store where the weaving was conducted the crowds were so great around the loom where Mrs. Fox worked that a space had to be roped off and policemen placed on guard to hold back the eager spectators. The Boston papers carried stories of the weaving and pictures of the women, the loom and the cabin interior where the demonstration was taking place. "The same people came day after day," said Mrs. Owenby, "and they never seemed to tire of watching Mrs. Fox at her work and of hearing her talk about her home in the mountains."

At Ease In The City.

Mrs. Fox is a typical example of a Southern mountain woman. Born and reared in an isolated cove in the Smoky mountains, she had never been outside her native county, nor had she ever been on a train, before last fall, when she made the trip with Mrs. Owenby to Boston. Strong of body, keen of mind, and skilled of hand, Mrs. Fox was as much at home in the crowded Boston store as she is in her own log cabin. She was not the least embarrassed by the strange city people she met and talked with them in her simple, naive manner about people and things at home. Dressed in a clean homespun frock that came almost to the floor, she told about her children, her husband, and her

—Cuts by Knoxville Engraving Co.

Above, Mrs. Riley Fox spinning on the porch of her home at Walden's Creek in the shadow of Mt. LeConte.

Below, Mrs. Allie Owenby, of Gatlinburg, who supervises the trips of the weavers and spinners to America's leading cities and tells

Eliza Goes to the City

Eliza Fox was an energetic woman who had her own horse and buggy and liked to travel. In 1929 this supreme weaver got a chance to go far beyond the Great Smokies to show how handwoven coverlets were made. In that year, she took her first train trip to demonstrate her skill in a Boston department store. In front of large crowds, she explained that weaving came as naturally to her as cooking, making lye soap, or dropping corn in "new ground." Before this more sophisticated audience, she worked in stocking feet, but at home Eliza always wove barefoot.

The following year, Eliza went on a more extended tour to stores in six large Midwestern cities. With her were her greatgrandmother's loom, along with spinning wheels and samples of coverlet masterpieces.

All the gear and materials were set up inside in a "faux" log cabin in the home furnishing sections of the stores. In a *Knoxville Sunday Journal* article showcasing the trip, the reporter wrote that people who weren't lucky enough to inherit handwoven coverlets were ready and willing to buy reproductions made by weavers. "The fame of the sturdy, honest, beautiful products from the looms of the mountain folk" had spread far and wide, and "wherever these wares are offered for sale, a ready market is always forthcoming."

And while Eliza and Josie Mast of Valle Crucis, North Carolina, demonstrated, Allie Owenby of Gatlinburg explained to onlookers how the weavers worked, the natural dyes they used, and other facts about the process. In a little bit of boosterism, Allie also passed around photographs of the newly created Great Smoky Mountains National Park.

The carved detail on Eliza Fox's spinning wheel reads "Anderson 1860." Eliza's granddaughter, Frances Fox, still owns the wheel.

heddles that hang on the harnesses. The warp was wound on the back-beam waiting to be advanced for weaving. For a coverlet, there could be 800 warp threads. The tension on the warp was adjusted, and the treadles tied.

The weft, or horizontal, threads were carried on a bobbin in the wooden shuttle that a weaver threw back and forth from one side to the other in the opening of the warp threads, called the shed. After each throw of the shuttle, the weaver pulled the beater bar forward to secure the warp thread in place. Pedal, throw, beat. Pedal, throw, beat. Over and over again in a steady, even rhythm, it would become almost a meditation. And then the miracle! Inch by inch, cloth began to form and a design emerged. Here was the weaver's reward for all her patience, organization, and careful attention to detail.

A traditional southern Appalachian coverlet was woven in a style called overshot, formed on a warp usually of plain weave white cotton, with a weft of wool in blue or red, though other colors were used too. In overshot, the weft threads skipped several warp threads and appeared to "float" on the surface. Within the overshot style, there were an array of intricate patterns—Catalpa Flower and Pine Cone Bloom, Chariot Wheel and Bonaparte's March, Blazing Star and Whig Rose, Lover's Knot and Tennessee Trouble, Cat Tracks and Snail's Trail, and what one author called the "quintessential overshot coverlet pattern," Sixteen Snowballs with Bowknot Border.

Each pattern required coordination of the loom foot pedals with the raising

Top: Walker sisters Hettie, Louisa, Margaret, and Martha pose for a 1949 Saturday Evening Post *article titled "Time Stood Still in the Smokies."*

Bottom: A woven hand towel from the Walker Sisters Collection.

of particular warp threads, following a specific pattern a weaver kept in front of her on the loom. These patterns, or "drafts," were long narrow strips of paper inked with marks that looked like a musical score. Like quilt patterns, drafts were often copied, shared, and passed down from one generation to the next. Drafts were rolled up and stored away, to be rediscovered years later, fragile and yellowed with time. But they still show the small pin pricks a weaver made to keep track of her place in case she was interrupted by some other chore.

The old four-harness hand loom—which was actually foot-powered—was the workhorse of mountain weavers. Built of heavy, rough-hewn timbers, the loom was a tool "like a plow," said Frances Fox of Gatlinburg. And it took up about as much room in a small log cabin. Looms were set up indoors

Tools of the trade: (clockwise from left) a boat shuttle, niddy noddy, and bobbin.

Whig Rose, a traditional pattern in an overshot weave.

in the winter, out on the porch in the summer, or in an outbuilding called a loom house. When not in use, they were taken apart and stored in the barn, hence the common name barn loom. People often bestowed a personal name to their loom too, based on who made it. "A McCarter," for example, referred to one built by local carpenter Eli McCarter. A four-harness loom allowed a weaver to make a piece of cloth about forty-four inches wide. To weave a coverlet big enough for a bed, two pieces of that width were needed, and they were then sewn together. A perfectly matched seam was a tribute to a weaver's skill. A neat straight edge, or selvedge, on the finished cloth, and a high number of shuttle crossings per inch of material were also points of pride.

For Frances Fox, weaving "is an unbroken line." Both her grandmothers were weavers. Eliza Fox, her paternal grandmother, lived on Waldens Creek at the foot of Mount Le Conte. She inherited a spinning wheel (inscribed "Anderson 1860") and wove on a barn loom. Eliza only wove coverlets, one for each of her children, earning enough money selling them in the 1930s to put three of her eleven daughters through college. Frances's other grandmother, Sarah Reagan, grew up in the Roaring Fork area, and made enough money from her weaving to buy an electric washing machine during the Depression. Sarah, said Frances, always kept cash in the pocket of her petticoat. For her, weaving was an occupation; for Eliza "it was her calling."

It wasn't until 1980, though, that Frances started weaving herself. She resurrected the old family loom her mother brought her, took a class at Arrowmont, wound her first warp around two kitchen chairs, wove a set of placemats, and thought "that would be the end of it." But Frances took to weaving like a bee to blossom. "I found my niche," she declared. She then worked for three years as assistant designer in the cottage weaving industry, studying under master weaver Nella Cook Hill. It was the same group her grandmother had woven for fifty years earlier. Frances came away from that experience seeing nearly infinite avenues of weaving open to her. Now in her studio in the Smokies Arts and Crafts Community, she keeps six looms going

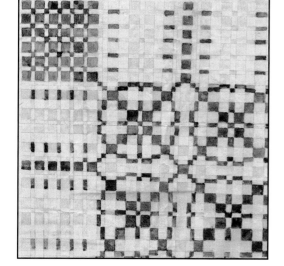

Chariot Wheel pattern (left) and draft.

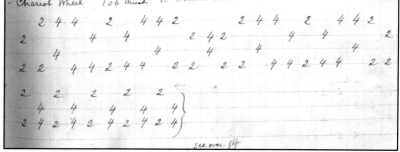

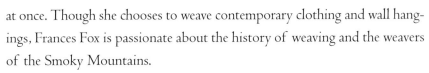

A four-harness barn loom housed at the Folk Art Center on the Blue Ridge Parkway. The weave pattern displayed is the Double Bow Knot.

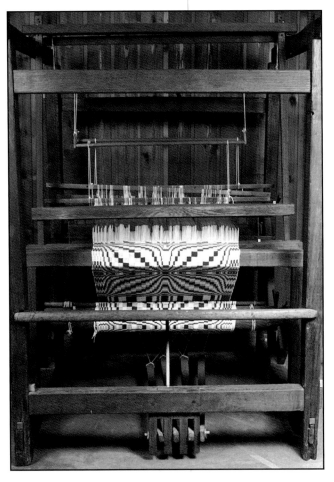

at once. Though she chooses to weave contemporary clothing and wall hangings, Frances Fox is passionate about the history of weaving and the weavers of the Smoky Mountains.

That history must include the weaving program of the Pi Beta Phi Settlement School in Gatlinburg. In 1912, the Pi Beta Phi sorority located their school near where Baskins Creek joins the Little Pigeon River. With a primary aim of educating children, it also became a center for weaving. The school found mountain weavers making quality overshot coverlets of linen and cotton and wool, a craft that went back several generations among Smokies residents. So they encouraged weavers to take it up again, to make money to supplement their families' subsistence farming.

Winogene Redding arrived at the Pi Phi school in 1925 as the weaving instructor. The little town of Gatlinburg, she wrote, "could not boast of a lawn mower, baby carriages, church every Sunday, [or] coal or electric stove...." Travel in and around the Smoky Mountains was still rudimentary. Redding, a tall, vociferous Canadian, would sometimes walk twenty-five miles in a week or ride a horse to go visit weavers. Soon she got an automobile, which might or might not have been an improvement in navigating the rocky, muddy roads. Within a year, "Gene" Redding had thirty weavers signed on to the program. But the weavers were an independent lot—insisting on working at home and selling by the piece.

In the Smokies, old family looms were brought out of barns, weavers took assignments, got yarn from the school, and proceeded to weave as time allowed. When they finished a number of pieces, they brought them in, got paid on the spot, took more yarn, and returned home to weave some more. Izora Keeler walked three miles and crossed Baskins Creek seventeen times to bring in her weavings. Cora Morton started weaving with the program when she was seventeen years old, and stayed with it for forty-seven years. After she was married, Cora would walk a dozen miles down from Cove Mountain, carrying a baby in her arms, to deliver her completed work.

As the Pi Phi program grew, at least ninety weavers were employed at any one time. Many made less than $150 a year, a few twice that. By the hour, it averaged between 45 to 50 cents an hour for the weavers, which doesn't sound like much for such skilled work, but it was more than minimum wage,

Below: The weaving building at the Pi Beta Phi Settlement School.

At right: Rebecca Ann Ogle Oakley weaving at a loom, 1937.

Above: Elizabeth Cogdill Reagan, known as "Aunt" Lizzie, weaving at the Pi Beta Phi School. She was 75 years old at the time of this photograph and earned her living by weaving.

At right: Pi Beta Phi Settlement School weaving instructor Winogene Redding (on right) with La Delle Allen, Arrowcraft manager, in 1925.

and during a time when the nation was mired in the Great Depression. People were able to buy things like home appliances that others in the country couldn't afford.

Early on, coverlets accounted for a greater share of the production. They sold for about $40.00 and took one to four weeks to weave (not including all the setup). But by the 1920s and 1930s, the weaving program shifted away from these larger, more expensive pieces to more salable and less time-consuming items—towels, potholders, baby blankets, and the popular Whig Rose placemats that sold for $1.25. Still, between 1936 and 1944 weavers made some 200 coverlets, but that was compared to literally tens of thousands of the smaller souvenir items.

The Loom Room at Pi Beta Phi Settlement School, 1929.

As Philis Alvic detailed in her book, *Weavers of the Southern Highlands*, many well-known Gatlinburg names appeared in Arrowcraft earnings lists—Clabo, Carver, Husky, Maples, McCarter, Ownby, Reagan, and Watson. Lucinda Ogle wove at the Pi Phi school from age eleven to seventeen. She came from four generations of weavers, including her grandmother Lucinda Bradley Ogle and her mother Rebecca Ann Ogle Oakley, wife of famous mountain man Wiley Oakley.

In the mid 1930s, with the creation of the national park, Gatlinburg's population quadrupled, the highway from Knoxville was built, and visitors flocked to the mountains. The Pi Phi Arrowcraft shop and several other outlets in town were selling handcrafted items, including weaving. A weaver's guild met regularly, and the women even wrote and produced original plays

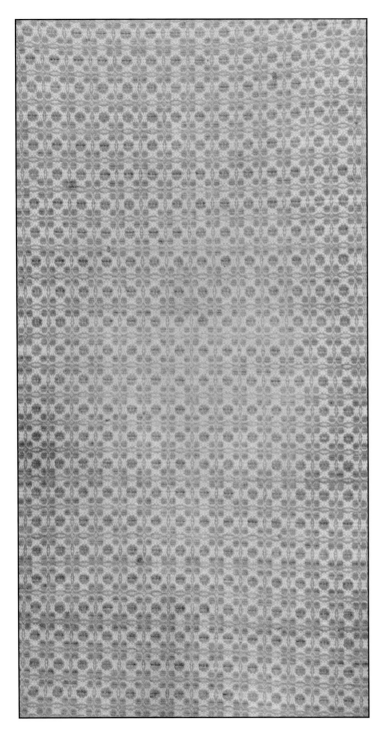

for the summer tourists. Lula Mae Ogle's "Store Britches: A Story of Way Back Yanner," was performed seventeen times in 1941 and featured old-time mountain speech and traditional harp singing.

Yet for many weavers it wasn't economics that inspired them to create coverlets. They made them as gifts for their children and grandchildren, kept them for special occasions, and undertook them out of sheer love of the form. In her classic book *Mountain Homespun*, Francis Goodrich told of one of the best weavers she knew in North Carolina, who was still producing coverlets "in her eightieth year." The woman said "she would choose nothing different than to weave on, were she to live her life over again. 'It is so pretty to see the flowers come out,' for it is as flowers that the design shows itself to the happy thrower of the shuttle."

Similar words would likely be uttered by many a weaver in the Great Smoky Mountains.

A woven cradle coverlet from the GSMNP collection.

THE WHITE HOUSE
WASHINGTON

December 8, 1933

My dear Miss Goodrich:

Miss Shanks has written me that you were responsible for the quilt which I so much admired at the exhibit of Southern mountain handicraft at the Corcoran Art Gallery last month, and I want to tell you now interested I was in all that Miss Shanks told me, not only about the quilt but in connection with the whole development of hand work.

The quilt was a work of art in design, in color, and in workmanship, and I cannot help but think that making anything as lovely as that would be a satisfaction to anyone who worked on it.

Very sincerely yours,

Eleanor Roosevelt

Above: Francis Goodrich, author of Mountain Homespun, *in 1943 with Double Bow Knot and Pine Cone Bloom coverlets.*

Right: A 1933 letter from Eleanor Roosevelt to Francis Goodrich.

THE WHITE HOUSE
WASHINGTON

Miss Frances Goodrich
Care Business and Professional
Women's Club

Asheville
North Carolina

READINGS

Alvic, Philis. *Weavers of the Southern Highlands.* University Press of Kentucky, Lexington. 2003.

Eaton, Allen. *Handicrafts of the Southern Highlands.* Russell Sage Foundation, 1937. Dover Publications 1973.

Holstein, Jonathan. *The Pieced Quilt: An American Design Tradition.* Galahad Books, New York. 1973.

Irwin, John Rice. *A People and Their Quilts.* Schiffer Publishing, Atglen, Pennsylvania. 1984.

Ramsey, Bets and Merikay Waldvogel. *The Quilts of Tennessee.* Rutledge Hill Press, Nashville. 1986.

Roberson, Ruth Haislip, ed. *North Carolina Quilts.* University of North Carolina Press, Chapel Hill. 1988.

Waldvogel, Merikay. *Soft Covers for Hard Times: Quiltmaking & The Great Depression.* Rutledge Hill Press, Nashville. 1990.

Wilson, Kathleen Curtis. *Textile Art from Southern Appalachia: The Quiet Work of Women.* Overmountain Press, Johnson City, Tennessee. 2001.

Wilson, Sadye and Doris Kennedy. *Of Coverlets, The Legacies, The Weavers.* Tunstede, Nashville. 1983.

Fanny and Zillah Wilson piece fabric together for a quilt, ca. 1933.

Quilt Patterns

There are nearly as many patterns for quilt blocks as there are quilters. Included here are some traditional favorites: Eight-Pointed Star, Log Cabin, Wild Goose Chase, Tulip, Flower Basket, and Windmill.

In the old days, quilters made templates of whatever they had—newsprint, cardboard, sandpaper, or plastic—and they kept the templates so they could be used again.

The templates shown here are designed to make one block of a particular pattern. Using an appropriately-sized copy of the pattern page, cut out the templates, place them on the fabric with the grain, trace around each template with a sharp pencil, adding a 1/4" seam allowance around each piece, then cut out each piece. The number of pieces of each template to be cut is indicated with each pattern.

Pieces can be joined by hand with a simple running stitch, or with a sewing machine. Accurate cutting and stitching are essential, because mistakes tend to accumulate. Press seams flat, not open, as you go, before assembling the block.

The total number of blocks depends on the desired size of the finished quilt, and will determine the yardage you will need. Once all the blocks are done, lay them out and join, again with 1/4" seams.

The patterns offer suggestions of light, medium, or dark fabrics, but beyond that it is up to each person's creativity in the selection of the types of fabrics and positioning of solids and prints, and lights and darks.

The beauty of a patchwork quilt top was (and is) that quilters can use up lots of pieces from the scrap bag. Early mountain quilters often reused fabric from clothing, feed sacks, or other sources. The most common fabrics were calico, broadcloth, muslin, and shirting material, though some quilts were made of silk, wool, and corduroy if such could be had.

Once a full top is pieced, the quilt is ready to assemble. Lay out the top, then the batting, then the backing, and edging or binding if desired. Hand or machine quilt the three-layered "sandwich" together.

Please note that these patterns are intended for quilters who have some knowledge about assembling pieces once they are cut out. Beginners are urged to consult the many how-to quilting books available in libraries, shops, and online for more detail.

Right: Apple of Paradise appliqué quilt by Emma Wood ca. 1882, North Carolina.

Source: Patterns modified from *Early American Patchwork Patterns*, Carol Belanger Grafton, Dover Publications, New York, 1980. Used with permission.

Log Cabin

Color chart

1 (dk I)	2 (dk II)	3 (dk I)	4 (dk II)	5 (dk I)	7 (med.)	5 (lt I)	4 (lt II)	3 (lt I)	2 (lt II)	1 (lt I)

2 (dk I)
3 (dk II)
4 (dk I)
5 (dk II)
6 (dk I)
6 (lt I)
5 (lt II)
4 (lt I)
3 (lt II)
2 (lt I)

Number of pieces to be cut for each block

Piece 1............................1   dark I
Piece 1............................1   light I
Piece 2............................1   dark I
Piece 2............................1   dark II
Piece 2............................1   light I
Piece 2............................1   light II
Piece 3............................1   dark I
Piece 3............................1   dark II
Piece 3............................1   light I
Piece 3............................1   light II
Piece 4............................1   dark I
Piece 4............................1   dark II
Piece 4............................1   light I
Piece 4............................1   light II
Piece 5............................1   dark I
Piece 5............................1   dark II
Piece 5............................1   light I
Piece 5............................1   light II
Piece 6............................1   light I
Piece 6............................1   dark I
Piece 7............................1   medium

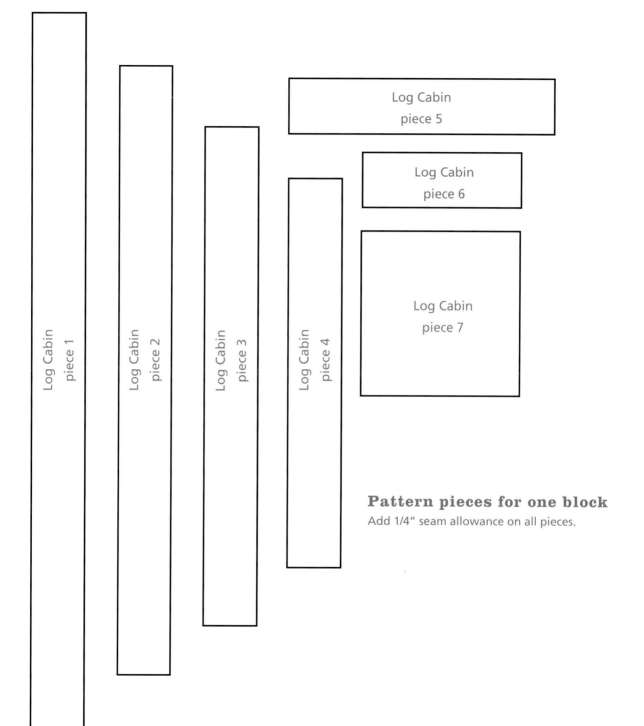

Log Cabin piece 1

Log Cabin piece 2

Log Cabin piece 3

Log Cabin piece 4

Log Cabin piece 5

Log Cabin piece 6

Log Cabin piece 7

Pattern pieces for one block

Add 1/4" seam allowance on all pieces.

Eight-Pointed Star

Color chart

	2 (med)		
1 (dk)	2 (lt) 2 (lt)		1 (dk)
	2 (med)		
2 (lt) 2 (med) 2 (med) 2 (lt)	1 (lt)	2 (lt) 2 (med) 2 (med) 2 (lt)	
1 (dk)	2 (med) 2 (lt) 2 (lt) 2 (med)		1 (dk)

Number of pieces to be cut for each block

Piece 1.............................1   light
Piece 1.............................4   dark
Piece 2.............................8   light
Piece 2.............................8   medium

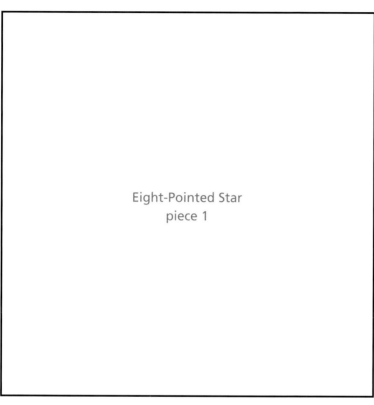

Eight-Pointed Star
piece 1

Pattern pieces for one block
Add 1/4" seam allowance on all pieces.

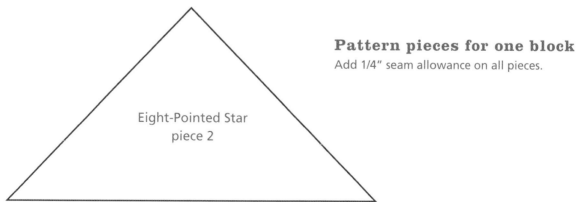

Eight-Pointed Star
piece 2

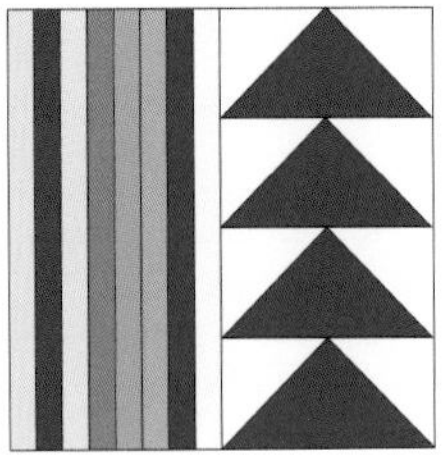

Wild Goose Chase

Color chart

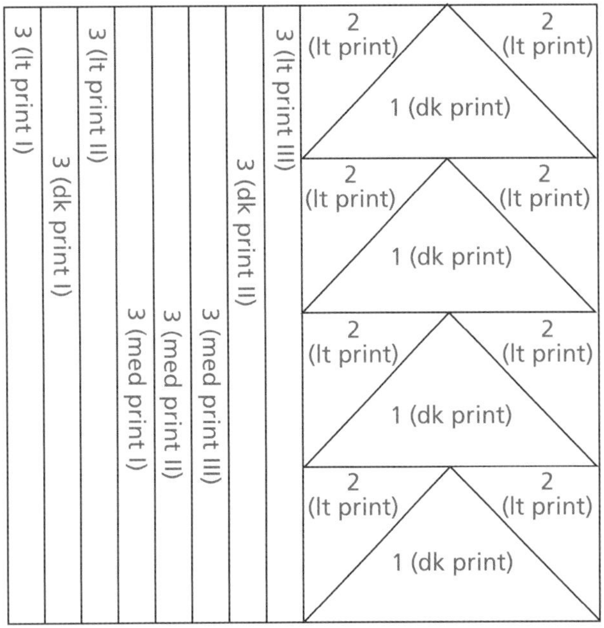
3 (lt print I)
3 (dk print I)
3 (lt print II)
3 (med print I)
3 (med print II)
3 (med print III)
3 (dk print II)
3 (lt print III)
2 (lt print)
2 (lt print)
1 (dk print)
2 (lt print)
2 (lt print)
1 (dk print)
2 (lt print)
2 (lt print)
1 (dk print)
2 (lt print)
2 (lt print)
1 (dk print)

Number of pieces to be cut for each block

Piece 1	4	dark print I
Piece 2	8	light
Piece 3	1	light print I
Piece 3	1	light print II
Piece 3	1	light print III
Piece 3	1	med print I
Piece 3	1	med print II
Piece 3	1	med print III
Piece 3	1	dark print I
Piece 3	1	dark print II

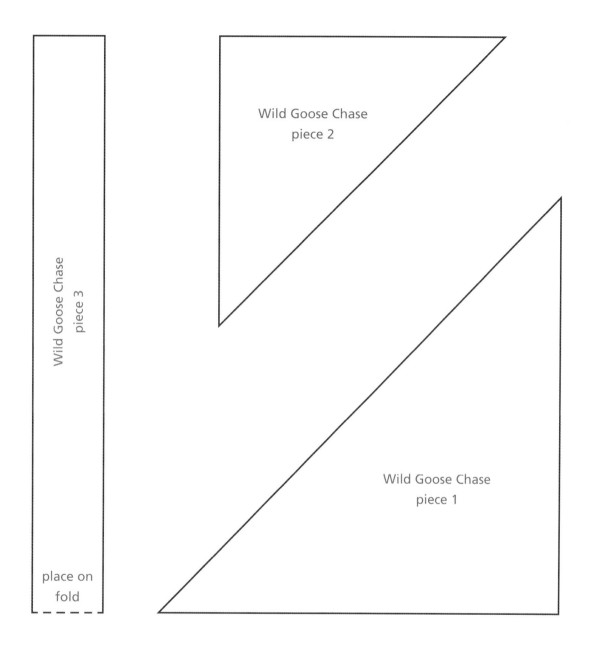

Wild Goose Chase
piece 2

Wild Goose Chase
piece 3

place on
fold

Wild Goose Chase
piece 1

Pattern pieces for one block
Add 1/4" seam allowance on all pieces.

Windmill

Color chart

1 (lt)	1 (dk)
1 (dk)	1 (lt)
1 (lt)	1 (dk)
1 (dk)	1 (lt)

Number of pieces to be cut for each block

Piece 1.............................4   light
Piece 1.............................4   dark

Windmill
piece 1

Pattern pieces for one block
Add 1/4" seam allowance on all pieces.

Flower Basket

Color chart

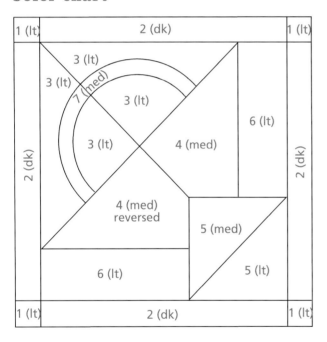

1 (lt)	2 (dk)	1 (lt)

3 (lt)

3 (lt)

7 (med)

3 (lt)

3 (lt)

4 (med)

6 (lt)

2 (dk)

2 (dk)

4 (med) reversed

5 (med)

5 (lt)

6 (lt)

| 1 (lt) | 2 (dk) | 1 (lt) |

Number of pieces to be cut for each block

Piece 1	4	light
Piece 2	4	dark
Piece 3	2	light
Piece 4	1	medium
Piece 4 reversed	1	medium
Piece 5	1	medium
Piece 5	1	light
Piece 6	2	light
Piece 7	1	medium

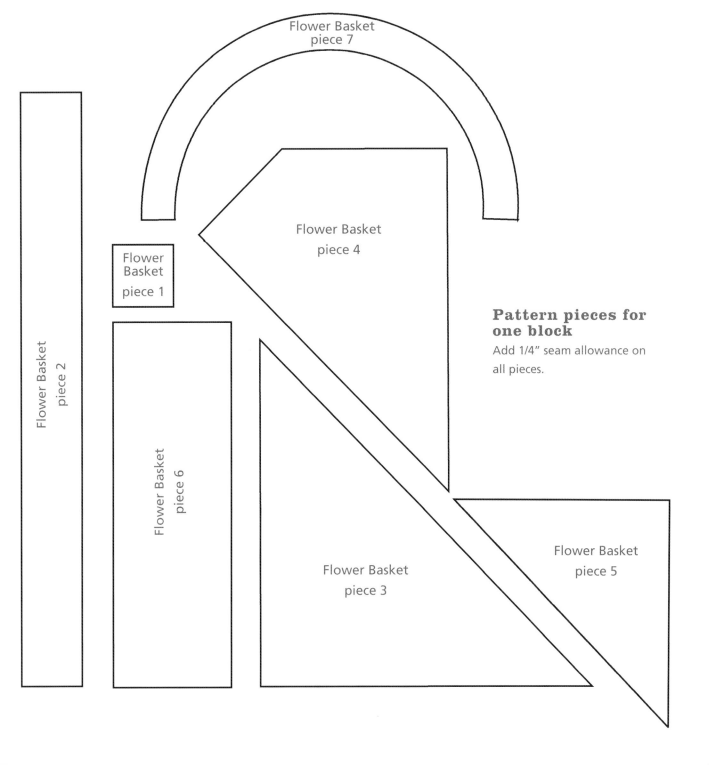

Flower Basket
piece 7

Flower Basket
piece 4

Flower Basket
piece 1

Pattern pieces for one block

Add 1/4" seam allowance on all pieces.

Flower Basket
piece 2

Flower Basket
piece 6

Flower Basket
piece 3

Flower Basket
piece 5

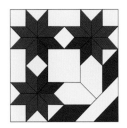

Tulip

Color chart

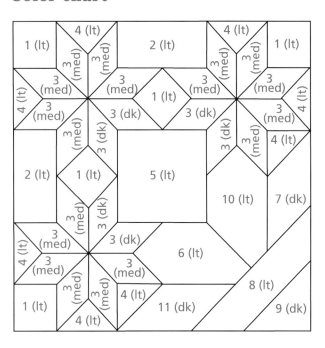

Number of pieces to be cut for each block

Piece 1............................5   light
Piece 2............................2   light
Piece 3............................18   medium
Piece 3............................6   dark
Piece 4............................8   light
Piece 5............................1   light
Piece 6............................1   light
Piece 7............................1   dark
Piece 8............................1   light
Piece 9............................1   dark
Piece 10..........................1   light
Piece 11..........................1   dark

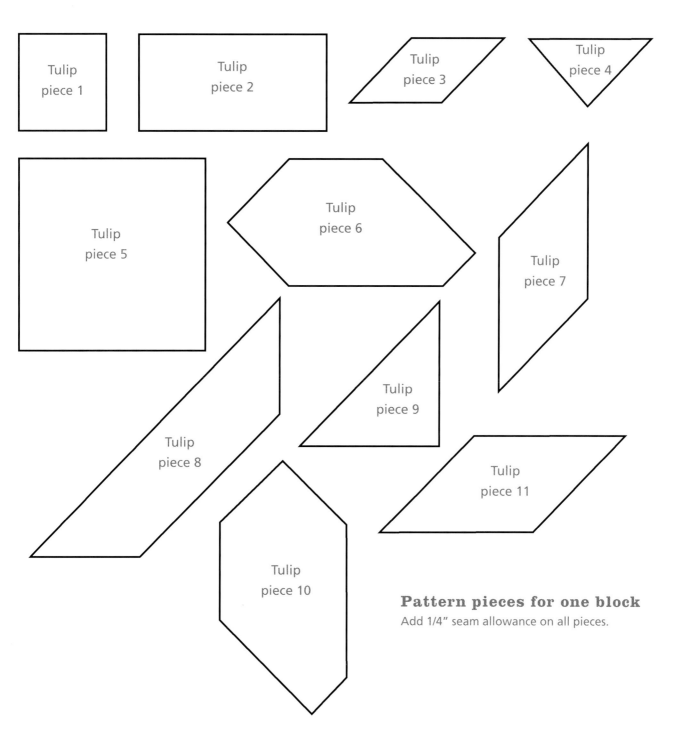

Tulip piece 1

Tulip piece 2

Tulip piece 3

Tulip piece 4

Tulip piece 5

Tulip piece 6

Tulip piece 7

Tulip piece 8

Tulip piece 9

Tulip piece 10

Tulip piece 11

Pattern pieces for one block
Add 1/4" seam allowance on all pieces.

ACKNOWLEDGMENTS

LIKE SO MANY OTHERS, I well remember the first quilt I ever made. I started embroidering the appliqué blocks when I was about ten years old, and will always remember doing some of them when I was in the hospital for surgery. Children don't forget such things. Then later, my mother and a friend finished the quilt, and it has come back to me, and hangs in a place of honor in my bedroom. In doing this project, I was struck how intimate quilts are, and how women didn't hesitate to invite me into their homes and into their bedrooms, where of course so many quilts live. And they openly shared so many stories, of their love for the craft and for family and friends, the fortunate recipients of their handiwork.

And so I want to thank them here, and hope I haven't forgotten anyone. To the quilters Ellen Ogle, Esta Laney and daughter Linda Stephenson, Iva McKee, Eva Myers, Maria Holloway, sisters Carol Huntley and Karen Nelson, who took me under their wings and showed me around, and Lila Wilson who got me started. Much gratitude to John Rice Irwin of the **Museum of Appalachia**, who, with his assistant Carol Ostrom, fed me lunch, told stories, and showed me many gorgeous quilts. Dianne Flaugh of the **National Park Service** opened the park's textile archives to me. Trevor Jones at **Western Carolina University** assisted in their collections, and Karen Green at **Arrowmont School of Arts and Crafts** was enthusiastic and helpful at every opportunity. Philis Alvic kindly offered comments on the manuscript, as did Julee Brown and National Park Service reviewers as well. I cannot begin to thank Frances Fox, who took many hours educating me about weaving, even letting me try my hand at one of her many looms. And to Steve Kemp at **Great Smoky Mountains Association**, for his constant interest in anything having to do with the Smokies, and for giving me full rein to explore another fascinating topic.

A Shoo Fly Pattern quilt from the Walker Sisters Collection.

PHOTOGRAPH CREDITS

Front and back cover: All images are from the Walker Sisters Collection, Great Smoky Mountains National Park archives.

David Luttrell: *13, 14, 17, 18 (Dutch Girl quilt), 19 (Spider Web quilt), 20, 21, 22, 23, 26, 28 (both images), 29, 32 (both images), 39, 45 (both images).*

The Doris Ulmann Foundation and Berea College, Berea, KY with special permission: *36 (Lizzie Reagan).*

John C. Campbell Folk School: *51 (Doris Ulmann photograph).*

Courtesy of Frances Fox: *38 (both images).*

Great Smoky Mountains National Park archives: *6, 7, 8 (cushion), 9, 12, 15, 16, 24, 25, 27, 31, 33, 36 (flax hatchel), 37, 40 (both images), 41, 42 (placemats), 46 (Rebecca Ann Ogle Oakley), 48, 67.*

Lewis Wickes Hine Collection, The National Archives: *46 (Lizzie Reagan).*

Courtesy of the Mountain Heritage Center, Western Carolina University: *8 (string quilt), 10, 34, 35, 36 (loom, Lover's Knot weave).*

North Carolina Quilt Project, courtesy North Carolina Museum of History: *18 (Bear Paw quilt detail), 19 (Carolina Lily detail), 53.*

Archives of Southern Highland Craft Guild: *5 (Doris Ulmann photograph), 30 (Doris Ulmann photograph), 35 (woman with dye pot), 36 (Elmeda Walker), 42 (Whig Rose pattern), 43 (both), 44, 49 (both images).*

Merikay Waldvogel and Betts Ramsey of Quilts of Tennessee Project, The Tennessee State Library: *18 (string quilt), 19 (Log Cabin detail).*

University of Tennessee Libraries, Knoxville (From Pi Beta Phi to Arrowmont Photographic Collection): *46 (Weaving building and image of Winogene Redding), 47.*